BLACK

RACKET

OCEAN

BLACK RACKET OCEAN

KAT DIXON

Poetry will be made by all!

89Plus and LUMA Foundation

0027 / 1000

First Printing: February 2014

ISBN 978-1-312-02571-4

LUMA/Westbau
Lowenbraukunst
Limmatstrasse 270
CH-8005 Zurich

Published by LUMA Foundation as part of the 89plus exhibition *Poetry will be made by all!* co-curated by Hans Ulrich Obrist, Simon Castets, and Kenneth Goldsmith at LUMA/Westbau, 30 January – 30 March 2014. Cover design by Content is Relative. All rights to this work are reserved by the author.

This book edited by Danny Snelson.

Series editor: Danny Snelson

Third Printing

Hush now, we're almost through.

PART ONE

In Seoul

Call it rose days, the stars are coming down.
He has black hair, he says to lie down

Like dead do,
Play dead as one corpse or another

Within these four gates. All stars come down.

I still like the sound of the world when it's moving
To move you.

Anyway, I didn't
Fall into or out of the ocean, I didn't leave

The way I could have, on a train. He has black
Eyes for remembering dead. He says to lie down.

There's a handful of ways to remember me –
Blue dressed, little sister, fireworks. Girl gone

Down. These are our rose days, the east gate

Gone out of a compass, gone

Silent as any one corpse. He has me.

I no longer remember
Any words in the language my language

Twinned from. Stars coming down from the mouth.
These fast minutes are for rose days –

Don't speak, little sister, not even of the dead.

I didn't leave the way I could have, in a blue dress.
We're so quiet, we're dead

Lying length to length on the bed. He has
Black hair, he makes stars

Come down where the east gate was
When there was a place such as that.

Look, White Curtain, Drag the Floor

Anyway, we were inside the turning
over stomach called a wave and then,

for quiet, out on top of the roof again
as ourselves. I held the light out

with my little hand. As yourself, you
were thinking about someone else,

and – that's it – I didn't mind being
with you then. I held the light out

with my little hand. Anyway, the ocean
wouldn't throw up anything but foam

that hour and big, ugly birds. A wave
came out of it and went under it

for quiet. A damn big, ugly bird. As
myself, I moved the floorboards.

Any other us might not know to walk there;
white curtains dragged. On the roof,

I turned your whole stomach, made foam.

A wave came out of it and moved

the floorboards. I was thinking about

someone else. No bird to cover up

the streetlamp, I held the light out

with my damn ugly little hand.

Everyone Wrote a Bomb

Come down now
We are coming down

Into the blue
Backward

Absolutely what you want
Sort of sound. Everyone,

Listen. Everyone,
Go ahead and write a bomb.

I was inside of it
I was inside a blue sweater

When the sea came in
The sea fat full of starfish

Little hands for where the people
Are

On the street
On the long fat street toward

The ocean
Coming down.

Maggie wrote the sound:
Big fat bombs, blue

Come down now inside
The seaweed

What you absolutely want.
Listen. Everyone,

Come down. Where the people
Are

Where the people are
On the street

On the street going backward

Little hands opened flat, fat

For the ocean

There is a sound.

For Luna

To say you are loud paper
I got lost in a taxi, on a bus,

On the streets of Siena,
In the brown and gray walls

Of Siena, I held a man's hand
Steady on my skin.

He didn't speak English, he opened
Me wide with a needle.

When it hurt, it did hurt,
How could I double my hurt

Into him in his language, a language
For needles, the brown or gray

Blood he took out me
Though they say you won't bleed

In Siena. Though they say I don't
Have blood in me at all.

He drew a bird with a needle,
He said: Kitty, okay? and words

Became walls the way they can
Become walls, the way some birds

Have needles for brains and needles
For wings and needles for girls

When girls go to paper, go loud.

Laced

When I become in love with you or anyone,
I'll know it. I am of the orchestration:

do you want to make plans like I want
to make plans? That's what all relationships are,

that's right. Being pushed out of or into
dog shit. Don't put that in a book –

you've already finished that book. I didn't want
to lose you. I didn't want to,

lost you. I was of the orchestration. I shape
look out so it won't fit in your ear.

Fruit

I think I am your welcome. Make a play and make it
last from here to the county line. There's nowhere left

for home: I've eaten all pies, all housewares resembling
pie. A dog won't bark, but I do not think I dreamed

those siren sounds – I was standing full up, I was rolling
flat crust for a pie. Nowhere for home, we had everyone one

of us come out of an airplane, having been shaped for
seats in an airplane in the model of fruit grown old-treed

for a pie. You're welcome, I think I am too, I am shy of an
exit, dry-eyed. Noah made a play out of fruit, and it turned

out to be very bad. As punishment, I wear peach-colored
clothing from here to the county line. I was rolling flat crust,

dry-eyed. Standing full up, we had every one of us come
out of an airplane, all housewares resembling pie. Having

been shaped for a dream, we were shy of an exit. Noah
made a play out of fruit, and an airplane came out of it.

I do not think I dreamed it, I had already eaten all pies.

Nowhere for home, I wore peach-colored clothing from

here to the exit, dry-eyed. Noah made a siren sound, we

were every one of us an airplane, having been rolled flat

as a pie. It turned out to be very bad. As punishment, I

think I am. There's nowhere left for home, you're welcome,

I was old-treed and shaped to be shy. We were every

one of us making a play out of siren sounds. I do not think

I dreamed an exit, I was rolling flat crust for a pie. All

housewares resembling siren sounds, we had every one

of us come out. I do not think we dreamed an airplane, we

were standing full up, dry-eyed. Noah, make a play and make

it last until there's nowhere left for siren sounds. A dog

won't bark. A dog won't bark from here to the county line.

(Little) Morning

Ringed two full years now, and to
What distances? We call that alone

Time: baking the pots we've stored
In the oven. When we turned

The sky out on one another, I was
Still underneath.

Typhoon Typhoon

I won't have it, I won't have
the usually returning dew.

I have a memory for infinite
tedium, keep

what you don't want to lose
away from me. See a boy

on a ship. See a boy on a wave
under a ship. In a house, it's a house

making moisture. The boy says:

No, he doesn't say that, I say
it to him. I made a poem, you

didn't ask if I made one or two
poems. He's in a city, in that city

there's threat of all sea.
No one around to participate

in my bad luck, I make for negative
geography. See a hand or two hands,

a voice or my voice
and the telephone, it's raining.

Sound or Something More

If I had learned how to paint
the big sad, I never would have

pretended to be in love.
I said

the words out loud, by way of practice –
to portraits in hallways, all blue

or all yellow; to cranes when
they went passing, hourly,

over the cul-de-sac in both directions;
to the windshield, the way it looked

along the Turnpike, covered in little flying bodies
more than glass;

to anything still brave enough to go
floral, the sofa in the unused

room; to books – to the smell
of books, to the smudgy mark

of fingers pushed into their creases;

to no one in particular or the addresses

of no one in particular;

to the ribbons in my hair. There was

some color I never could catch, some

combination. The canvas went away

and then I touched it.

We put walls inside of our walls.

Reptiles

G is insisting the covers be cleaned, the
curtains. How nice it is for you to have
become an initial. G won't step eyelash inside
the reptile shop because spiders and snakes
and, sure, I've slept with more people than
he has. Rachel and I are at the window of the
reptile shop, the iguana. The iguana has
made his spine out of other men's teeth.
G wants to know how anyone – how I – could
want a beach when he wants no beach. And
the washing machine and the washing machine.
Rachel and I are inside the reptile shop.
There are spiders and snakes in the reptile shop.

Right Through

Telephone told us
fire in the walls,

but the house was quiet-
quiet on arriving.

The car came and everything
else. Two forecasts

unfastened at the hip,
again where brother left

the bruise. Two hammer
shades of purple

and we hit it off
like matchsticks.

Poem Found Highlighted in Juan Rulfo's "Macario"
Purchased Used, September, 2012; or, I Shape Where You
Want to Remember, I Ruin

Godmother, frogs are green all over
except on the belly. Toads are black.

Godmother's eyes are also black –
Felipa has green eyes like a cat's

eyes; I love Felipa more than God-
mother, alone in the kitchen cooking

food for the three of us. I'm always
hungry

and I never get filled up – never.
They say in the street

that I'm crazy
because I never stop being hungry.

Go to church: she sets me down
next to her and ties my hands

with the fringe of her shawl. I do
crazy things – found me hanging

somebody, a lady, just to be doing it.
I don't remember.

People who invite me to eat
get close, throw rocks at me until

I run away.
Felipa's milk is as sweet as hibiscus

flowers; it's been a long time
since she has let me nurse the breasts.

She would fix the breasts so that I could
suck the sweet, hot milk; tickle me all over.

I wasn't afraid of being damned to hell
if I died there alone some night,

the fear of mine that I have of dying.
I'm full of devils inside.

Bar the door so my sins won't find me out.
Felipa says the crickets always

make noise

so you can't hear the cries of souls

suffering. Maybe there are more

crickets than cockroaches

among the folds of the sacks

where I sleep.

True Dialogue

He says you brought the smoke in with you this time
Because smoke can become a knitted scarf some days

Or the blue silk handkerchief in your front pocket –
Though usually it doesn't, usually you come in without it –

And don't do it again. So many planets were pulled
Into alignment, and we did not talk about it happening

Because we were suddenly still not dead. I think occasionally
About driving my gray Chevy into the little pond on Holt

Road where geese go to bring the planet smaller geese
And lead them crooked across the street in school hours.

It's an easy task, the more I think of it, the road's quick
Curves and soft shoulder, water up to the neck. I could

Say my eyes got caught in Christmas lights, my thoughts
Inside of any old, sad song on the radio, how they play

Old, sad songs at night on the radio when no one is awake
To be listening to the radio, all the DJs quiet somewhere

No one else has ever been to coding messages to one
Another across an unknown galaxy of sound. The more

I think about it, too, I have begun to carry smoke around
Like constant, steady breath or the nearly invisible coat

Of hair that comes with any skin and is so much a part
Of skin that it is safe to say that skin is more than just

The clumping up of individual, moving cells but also a clear
Forest, or, since I bother to shave most mornings, at least

A patchy set of woods. Whichever way I wear it, I have begun
To carry smoke, and it could very well be the reason why

The houseplants are dying. Dying not in the way we blame
Winter for but by something more akin to leprosy or the levels

Of rashes too unsettling to show in slides in the back chapters
Of the medical textbooks your grandfather gave to you

So that you might understand how horrible and ugly it can be
To be alive. Tell me, how can I begin to apologize for that?

Maybe if I drive my gray Chevy into the little pond on Holt

Road, where the geese have come and gone by way of season

And the shoulder still is soft and soggy from the water crawling
Misty-eyed like planets through the grass up to the pavement,

And by some luck I can outlast the flooding, if I leave the window
Cracked enough to swim through in my white coat, or by new

Chance the airbags float my Chevrolet to safety on the opposite
Good shore, I could walk the night to one of my old houses

Or to yours.

Like Speech

you are
when you aren't

attending to
beach we go

and back   what
did you say

or mean waves
        when they strike

one or two rolling

bodies and all the right
words

where you left
unpunctuated in sound

We Go to the Big Telescope to Witness the Death of Some Faraway Star

We went to the big telescope –
It wasn't dark.

If I remember what you remember
It wasn't dark. There were only everywhere

Trees. Radio told us: devastating event.
It doesn't matter, you said, that all we can see

Are trees.

We went to the big telescope
And crawled inside the big telescope

How someone might slide inside an X-ray.
It was dark.

Radio told us: somewhere the death.
Somewhere the devastating

So devastating event. You crawled inside

I crawled inside

Broken black inches of X-ray.

I'd meant to ask
If looking down the eye of the big telescope

Would be more like the whirlpool
Or the hollowed out bone.

Inside the sad crackling radio, no space
Could match the personal effect

Of downing
Or of choking on a lazy tongue,

But oh how many times I've been wrong before.

We went flat inside the X-ray
And told ourselves we could see more

Than our own eyelashes. It was so devastating,
The dark.

It might take a long time, you said,
For the star to die. It might be so stubborn.

It might take its whole life. I knocked
My cold knuckles against my available bones

To be sure they weren't your bones.

If I love you I can't begin to say
I miss my language. I can't begin to say.

In the fish-eyed world of the telescope,
Scenes of dark matter went on being over-

Shadowed by scenes of dark matter.
I expected the lonely hiss of black holes,

Anything to bring us back to beginning
Again.

But big black holes are quiet.
That's not, you said,

The devastating event.

PART TWO

Break Glass to Extinguish

Killing is a thing we do in measure,

One by one. The sunflower first –

We display in bit-lip pride to

Relatives and company come full

Starch. Aunts look on its molding

Vertebrae for laughter, clutched

And clawed at, like the end of last

Year's favorite anecdote. Friends

And other visitors pinch

Browned and barnacled leaves

For souvenirs to say we've grown

A thing that would not live.

The dog, with its own unmatched

Skeleton, is something more

Of a loosed grenade. The stitching

Of its pink and slept-with elephant

First must separate

To reveal the powdery tooth fillings

That birds will use in winter

To cushion themselves against an

Over and over cold spell. The food,

In heaping handfuls of anything already

Dead, must wrongly expire. A holocaust is

Where we fit our hands

Around that hound's pinched middle

With our increasing tightness until the only

Weight is what emptiness can

Be amassed inside one once alive

Creature. We clean the bones in

White vinegar and, with dried beans,

Fill to half whole one milk jug to make songs

For the funeral parade and home again.

The sound is steady beating like a year

Lived to end in any unloved place.

When I'm lucky – in dreams,

Alone – nine or so lovers

You took once or longer

In various seasons of summer

Or rain and all the unofficial

Women you pressed in fantasy or

Memory onto the pages of one

Red notebook, perfectly bound,

Make lovely, arching swan dives

Off of cliffs or rooftops or

Any other precipice high enough to turn

A stomach into circles within its own

Casing. Their necks go cracking and skin,

And I am free of them enough to stretch

Awake in sheets that must be

Burned to unfasten their mistake.

And love, when it comes time for its

Undoing, is not nearly half the trouble.

I Am Slow as the World

Are you sorry for what will happen? There

are so many months that I've spent stealing

other women's poems, the moon. I do

not think so, I do not think you will come

upon a single calling

of I do. I am a great event when I walk in

in one lace dress that went purchased before

threat of it, even before there was a man

to say he would, I do. I rehearse you,

small white sheets or bath

hours but do not have to happen when you

say or I say I do. He is arranging his small

brown poems. He stands on the hills, one

pleasant-appearing thing and then another. I

am ready, I do

what I already know. What happens in me is

a thing that happens without need or want of

attention – the moon comes faced as

a man – but I do.

Bride Flight

Twelve down, twenty down on the bank

and back heavy; unusually winged.

Half-bodied now and buzzing, two

or two climb past remember, past

recognition into that blue summer

month in which lakes split their beds,

open-mouthed.   Honey-touched,

drone by drone will sky march

to a falling, but now – oh, follow – can't you

hear the beating of a flight pattern? None

still-sitting on the lawn. Out and out

to that fresh grade, to that now singing

palisade where dead relatives once

walked, hand-locked and wet behind

the ears. Where my mother went when

I laid murder to her in a dream –

bibulous and sunk for years.

Linden Tree

If I could keep this: this linden tree feeling

when all-time melts into one stiff driveway

and I can only fold a love song into telephone

lines. There's a satellite that will take me any-

where to you. The way a map opens, lifelike,

and grows to make a system out of any speck

of land makes each day spent without you

seem like any minute someone will inform

me that I've been walking around with so

many broken bones.

Simple Love Song on the CD You Left in My Car

Let's skip everything and lie here, lie in bed.
I have so many pairs of panties it's incredible,
it's actually

incredible, this is not an invention. Let's lie in
bed and be difficult. Let's do anything that
involves lying

in bed. Lisa wants to know how it will be
when we're only ever driving through tunnels.
We're in a tunnel

when she says it, how will it be, and surely it
won't last for always. Surely there are ways
of shortening

this map I have of you and where you are,
how far I can get with my hands before you
open up, your

lazy mouth and all of you. Like maybe I didn't

cut these fingernails, I left

the shell of them inside of you. You're in

my gray shower, you're lying in bed. Your

feet and still the shape of them,

you're lying in bed. Lisa counts

the yellow signs for caution:

Use your headlights a tunnel is coming it is

it's a tunnel turn on every little light

you can. We're in bed, we are,

I hit the last whisky switch, we're

underneath the ceiling fan.

Paint-Painted & A China Doll

1.

You are I am rudely

      awoken by blueberries; make your
predictions.

Any textbook begins meaning
stab yourself seven times in each organ

for luck.   Here's what I know about not
knowing you.

2.

See here signs of misplacement at or during
birth.

I unpack the boxes: buttons, eyelashes,

people going home,

      bird of felt feathers,

a book of you

when you weren't yet tipsy on rum and less
fatal

          diseases.

Explain that again. You do.

3.

I put what I remember where I remember.

See how half of the flowers are

          unremarkably
dead.

      For a poem, I wouldn't dare

make you as beautiful as you are.

Bang Bang

I was not responsible:

Green copper residues remembers

rain happened here.

In the post-intellectualized mess of

eating peaches, feet and legs

aimed at perpendicular, too young for

a generation, Aleksey scrolls

his reasons for reconstructing

shipwrecks on the stairs

we've left unpainted.

A Letter

Here is the secret: I won the spelling

bee by mistake. Who could arrange

letters in those small bones? I hardly

hold onto my name. I hold onto the skin

around your waist. You are

selling my name to the skyline –

the skyline means cutting our view

of the sky. L-I-N-E. It's the same with love:

I mean when men decide to love me.

Who are you? I can't begin to count

the number of your white or yellow bones.

Blown Switch

I am waiting for a better crisis: don't you

know what I would see in you if I could learn to see

in the dark? It is middle into night the way

of the blown switch, the way of being hung up

midsentence on the inside of a black

turtleneck. The one I wear when it's too winter

for anyone to see me wearing anything in the loud

hurt of having to breathe in so much cold air. I want

to say to everyone *just close your eyes.* Anyway,

there's wind, there's no reason to be posed looking

into any one direction. A switch blows and

you are the dark when it refuses to end. After all,

there is no you – I am myself inside a turtleneck,

a crisis. I have closed and will keep closing my eyes.

Early Late Riser

Slashed at the arm, I know you, how you

    Poem. I hope you

Wake up in this timeline again. To receive

    A compliment

I want to make myself the opposite of that.

    A sound stops

Brief of a door or were there two sounds.

    The sour smell

Comes up again in my same chest – can you

    Believe I wrote

The same house as your house and the same

    Chest as my

Chest in it because I could never, I could

    Never hear the ocean

The way the ocean hears the ocean.

To receive a compliment

You walked out toward the ocean, made a

Poem. I hope you

Wake up. The opposite of that, I slashed

Myself at the arm.

If the Woman Is Told

If the woman is told she is crazy
after so many years in one marriage

is she crazy still? I went crazy
when told I'd turned twenty, when told

I'd turned. I was crazy before that,
maybe, I was maybe crazed. To become

twenty meant to become a woman,
which of course meant to come up

dressed in women's clothing, to come
up for air, from underneath

any man, any man-sized creature coming
into what could be a man, like church,

like sea breeze, gentle, dead melody.
It did not mean to kill all the men,

to kill what men would make me, a woman,

to kill what men would have me say.

Zelda

If you believe it the way she tells it, she
married him

because she'd heard somewhere that
married people

never go to jail. What remains
of the bubble bath sucks at her body like dry

skin.
Everywhere, he is. Everywhere he is

he is knocking on some windowed part of
her, he is touching in her some memory he

put there.

He speaks in books to other women,
color-coded.

Little Robberies

Relive me on a stone-capped floor, bone-

open and cracked hot of any bristling. Hot-

down and too many, midsummer or not.

Aunt Sarah, growing and dead, you and your –

and mine too, every bathtub, every two-

part door. Hungering in your wine-wear,

handwriting clumped at the uneasy. Every

crowded detail breaking at the nail. Won't

church-stop at any late hour. Won't outrun

the intersection – even chin-chapped, even

kissed somewhere else.

To Shore

I wanted to go to the waterfront,

sure, I wanted. Some on the boat said

This is a girl who knows what a poem

is supposed to feel like

only there wasn't a boat. We were

walking the ice to Mackinac, we were

Omaha up to the ears. I wanted to know

who you were, so I learned how to read.

Captain said Go down into the belly and flip

the second switch, and that was what it

meant to know sound in terms of shape –

the body in clothes or other consonants,

any open-closed mouth – because

before there was shape there was the ocean,

which was the thing I wanted, and that part

turned out to be true.

I Am Not at Home

The snow won't come to stay: too warm,

the roads, the homes, they say. I whiten

for the sheets, dismay, and all around

the memories go places where your hair's

gone gray, white places that are sick but stay.

I go, I am not quiet. Other men do not

touch me. They have been natural, they have

gone away. It is these faces that I mind:

children who are quick in play, importance,

lights that are too swift to end some winter's

day. Other women seek Holy in societies this

way. Let us flatten, launder, fade to gray.

What a Jealous Look

Look, I am this frantic misshaping of words. I
Can't tell a truth. I want to love you.

Far off, an ocean sacrifices girls for white
Beach. I last as long as I need to.

I am not – I am not a solid ticking of clocks.
I color my hair beige, I am not an artist.

Look, I am not. I will not be hospital. I want
To make a comma mean something more than

Take a breath.

October

Every following car is someone to be lost.

It takes so many hours of daylight to convince

Oneself that love can happen and only

So much nighttime to know it won't. Of every

Man and woman, girl and boy we've touched

There are strangers

Still, before and after everything else.

I found one of yours in a book

And then another. I found one of yours

In a bar, looking like Halloween

(though August, I tell you, who could forget)

With a hand shoved into mine like a cigarette

From a stranger outside the bar after

Where I waited to be told Forever. I love you

Forever. I found one of mine

In the aftermath bath time – and another –

By way of hello. I found one

Of the ways I still love you stinging in morning-

Time, there at the knife-ready stop

Light where all the best roads meet and pass

One another in the fashion played forward

By my stiff and remembering heart.

Clean

I excite: a sleep in sheets unshowered,
Laundry on the floor. The dog

Becomes a dream of your skin against
My skin the way it was in Pompano –

I never learned to spell, never learned away
Your morning smell. Never

Fell out of a love song or onto the rug.
There's such a thing as too much

Symmetry. On the stairs, you fit your whole
Hands around my throat and

Wasn't that a feat, wasn't that an in-between.
This is what a man does,

That's what you said. I peeled tangerines and
Fit them into your closed

And angering mouth. How disgusting, that's

What you said, but you meant

My face, the loose river of it, the sorry

Field where nothing

Stays. How disgusting, that I became

A summer where everything lives

Lesser, shrinking daisies in the vase. Why

Inflate my heart when you won't

Come? Whatever crude shape of me, I resume

My sex and dream my unwashed

Self a love that doesn't alphabetically spell

Goodbye.

Psychosis

What a lonesome day you've chosen for us.

    Remnants

of Florida begin to disappear: the mascara

    runs dry, shoes

begin to crack at the creases. I am not the

    same girl who

feared the outside at night or any unfamiliar

    set of eyes.

I fear words and how they start to mean

    other words.

The sky is a landing strip

    when I run

out of things to say. Look up. I am through

    with talking

about the way I feel. There are so many

    planets – how many

are smaller than I am? How many fill themselves

    to the brim.

Last Poem

You're the you in this poem,

the one where I'm dead in the orange room,

the one where I'm dead abroad. In this poem,

I'm dead in a hospital room calling

coma with old lovers, calling languages

I can't remember speaking while awake.

You're the you in this poem. If we're both

what we should be, you'll be dead before I

come home.

PART THREE

Home (Reprise)

I will hear it come morning, the nothing sound

of deep-lunged pauses while you stir the tea,

of the slow quarter moon half-circling 'round,

caught once in the lattice work, pulled to the ground,

where doves collect rumors beneath the elm tree

and coo to dead lovers, a sweet nothing sound.

I anticipate: how do you do?, compound

sentences, sunflower seeds, nothing as free

as the slow quarter moon half-circling 'round,

so unlike the kettle, alarming, inbound

train pressing importance on activity.

I'll catch it, by morning, the old nothing sound.

Visitors, knocking, won't notice the dreams, found

by witch luck on two tongues, in the temblor sea

of the slow quarter moon half-circling 'round.

(Medicinal headaches, allergic, profound

learn nothing of weathervanes, nothing of me.)

I wait for it each morning, the nothing sound

of that slow quarter moon half-circling 'round.

Pele in Love

In these oceans, there is always the
possibility of disruption. Love is a heat that
begins south of here and warms the currents
going north again

all the way to the brink of borderlands,
where I sleep empty. There were times when
I burned alive whole men – on the street, in
their Sunday clothes,

on the way to other women,
buying shoes, buying dinner, buying me
drinks to cool down any given bar. Smoke
weaves

with skill into my socks, hair, sweater dresses.
Winter doesn't end anymore; rain starts
with me and covers several worlds. He
is picking out the

pieces left for stumbling inside my crater. He
is set for saving what is left of his old bones.
The moon is quartered, penniless, above my
peaks, and every

part of me knows how to be alone. I am
known for being the forgotten sister, blackened
now and then by my own acidic temperament
and where

we've been. He splinters wood against the
carpet; he tortures glass in every dropping
mood. I melt what's left of home with each
mislaid touch of skin

and ride the current northward, westward,
out and out to each new island I construct
with walls to seal my heart for murdering
another heart. Sailors and

other guests make passes to say How brave
we are! to meet the siren with open mouths
and travel on with lungs still full of steady

breath. I pull pages from

their books and leave them scattered for

some future haunting when I'm gone-gone

again and outward plunging where I make

my bed beneath the sea. He

won't see me anymore; he hides his whole

heart beneath a sweater. He once fell in love

with a set of sentences and that was all. What

shaped me into

lightning was the fullness of punctuation and

how an ending can come unexpectedly without

the downward curve of sound. I am a

poison left inside of you,

black and blackening. I am the native ghost

you save for rainy days and poems you won't

write to prove I've made contact with your

outermost constellations. I move

along the shoreline, wrinkling beaches into

rock – a fierce and tireless wave that cycles

fire through the veins of this lazy, melting

earth and breaks land from land in the moon-

light of a river night in which all hearts

are tricked and trick themselves into love.

Nightlight

I fill the space
between my fingers

outside Luna, New
Mexico with six billion

people, six petrified
monuments, all in one

stitching, so close I could
tuck them in a pill bottle.

Too, there were words
that never touched, though

I bought them at bargain
prices. Scott's goodbye

came with ribbons, *move*
fast enough and time no

longer exists. Six miles

to the Arizona border, I sold

my translations for an extra

hour of bodiless constellations.

Cinque Terre

The French boy spoke enough English to say

He didn't speak any English, so he broke his

Bread in two for me on the train. Outside the

Train said All best heavens are for anyone

Who won't speak English. I opened my

Mouth for the salted sea.

Place of quick lightning, I climbed the map

Now hundreds of steps. It wasn't the faulty

Translation. Dock down under Corniglia,

Wood on rock and away from every tall,

Sleeping human, went out like sad music into

Nighttime, into the warm-bodied sea.

The American boy said How strange to find

Another American. I put my tongue right into

The other side of flat Earth. On the slippery

Cliff said Everywhere some sick-lipped

American. He was quiet, how strange, he swam

Right away from me, deeper than I for the sea.

End of all land, Vernazza, colored for carnival –

I tripped back into the throat. What after all

Is water but steadier repetition of discordant

Sound. Tourists, all touring, talked their way

Into lines for the ferries, a treat to hover that

Way, one breath above the hungry sea.

The German girl was first to break the tide,

Little tooth. I went underneath the splash to

See it. She was *la la la*, pinker than sex drink,

Size of a pebble, drowned – no word in her to

Match the soft-swinging, vibrating noise of

Ocean shrinking, turning to sea.

Orca

When I grow up, I'll be the blocks and the city

when it's overflowing with light. I'll be the sea

when it surges; the steel of any towering bridge.

When I grow up, I'll still be the back of a hand

when it makes contact; I'll still be an apology

when none is needed. I cannot know exactly

when habits like these will begin to rot and ruin.

When I grow up, I'll be everything yellow-tasting

when I can be. I've never feared death except

when the threat came of a knife to the neck, even

when sleeping, even when there's no one around.

When I grow up, I'll be a map running into oceans

whenever you turn the page. I'll be dark blue night

when it is fog against the streets and steering wheels,

when it is keeping you away from home. Tell me,

when will I grow up to see the world and how and

when it is best tuned for spinning? I cannot say just

when, but I will be the friction that unsettles it again.

I Am Simple Again; I Believe in Miracles

I dream you where I left you, where was that.
There is no

bad habit, no burnt brain that can't be healed
with the right

hand or hour learned upon some pillow. I
call them friends when

they come to sit with me in the night. I'm
busy missing the way I used to fill a mirror

with my whole
heart. For you, there will always be the

gulley of some unshaved
thigh, and, sure, I'll go and go dead-safe

within some bloodied hive.
These are not acts of dreaming: I'm tired

of you becomes a sentence that still feels like

I want to fall asleep between your ribs.

Unexpected Confrontations with Smallness

[i.]

Little heart, I put words in you. I heard
you weren't ashamed to be alone.

In spring, I swallowed all the cherry petals,
put them in a wicker basket

for putting again inside of me, later,
when my watch had stopped – there were

at least as many as stars. No one came
to ask if I could breathe that way,

all the petals put down the throat,
the wicker basket suddenly emptied

save for strings of falling pollen,
how we all were, but as it turns out, yes,

I could. Little heart, I heard

you weren't ashamed to be alone.

[ii.]

When the watch stopped, I put words

in you. I mean, I put my teeth to nibbling

at your ear. I put my arms through the window

where the ivy hugged the lattice, hanging

(how we all were, in summer) thin-leafed

through similarly shaped mouths. Still,

the ivy would not bear to spin my name.

Sometimes magic won't work. Knowing that,

you put your hands in my hair. Not knowing

how to breathe, I put words in you,

but the small, right hands of the clock

would not go on spinning and it's as true

to tell you that I can't remember now

which words those were.

[iii.]

Little heart, I wouldn't give you any name.

I heard you fell out of a window or did you

jump. No one came to ask. In all the falling

pollen, one and then another must close

her similarly shaped mouth or else be asked

to swallow. To stop a watch, I climbed the cherry

tree and counted the white petals: how many

could fold to fit inside of me, how many

had come from inside of me and fallen out

the way we all had through the throat.

I wouldn't go to any hospital. Little heart,

I wouldn't give you any name. From my way

out of the window I could see all those damned

white petals – there were at least as many as stars.

Pele on the Mountain

If it weren't for fog and distance, one might

view the ocean turning somersaults from

here. I stretch to touch each edge of the

caldera with one of my

scorched limbs. Washington is next to blow:

its well-tuned timber makes a bed for smoke

to seep in sleep through every stunted nook

this state can hold within

its squared and watery borders. I float on the

backs of it. I've learned the trick from

fireplaces: how people invite danger into

their own homes. The spinning globe

is my divining rod for selecting where and

when to breathe ashes onto unsuspecting

towns and peoples, to watch them, mirrored,

grappling for the objects onto

which they've projected lives and loves. I

know no such things. I'll pursue and be

pursued for violation and that will be the

memory of what you've meant to me all along.

Leave a Mess

Leave the cigarettes unfinished when you go.

Leave summer still

To happen and all the leaves gone red or yellow

Sealed for keeping

After you've gone. Leave friends at dinners,

Holding places for you,

Empty chairs that won't be filled by talk or

Toasting in the quiet months

Since you have gone. Leave the kitten set for

Scratching messages

Into the skin, the wine still bottled, the doors

Blown open for visitors

And registries of cold. Leave love untold, the

Telephone still dead

And unaware that you have gone. Leave the

Wind in every ribcage,

Beating code to say that you have gone.

Leave airplanes ascending

Altitudes and clocks to be reset when you

Have gone. Leave

Skin underneath your fingernails for evidence

Of what has made you

Go. Leave the mouth of every stranger filled

With gossip at your

Leaving, every tooth tuned to departure, every

Standing, sitting,

Falling body well-tempered for goodbye.

Leave everything and every-

One you've touched with fingerprints to be

Washed clean of upon

Some future bath time or dusting. Leave the

Steady ironed outfits

Swinging softly inside doorframes and the

Laundry set to spinning

In the washer, dryer, tornado season where

It was when you had

Gone. Leave the furniture upended, every
Book and dish
And conversation bloodied and chipping
Paint against the wall. Leave

Handprints on your spouse's cheeks and
Handprints in the pockets
Of your favorite jeans when you are on the way
Out and going.

Leave words you've said, not to spark a cinema
Or any attentive
Undertaking in the guise of Where have you
Been? but an all-

Around Hello for any potential admirer who
Might slip a note of praise
Into your skull when other eyes have turned
To go. Leave all mistakes

For reckoning in figures now that you have

Gone. Leave no voice to say

Gone, gone away when you're out-out but

Have not yet gone.

Mary Oliver

Ask any poem and it will say

It is tired of being left in the woods.

I went to woods – all the way

To woods – and was still in my old

Shape, not wood-shaped as a wood

Would have me or poem-shaped as a boy

Would have me – should he know the shape

Of that old poem made of woods.

If there were fewer poems, it's sure

That there would be more woods

Or at least more paper airplanes we

Could use to travel by if we would

Go from wood to wood the shape

Of paper when it is laid out white

And plain for holding poems. In any

Poem I am white and plain as Mary

Oliver in a day for going to woods

And cutting woods into the shape

Of poems, if a wood could fit the page

For poems, as a poem is always squire

Like a city or rectangular like a city

And not meant to be natural and big

And alive as woods. I live in the city –

I will not go dead the way of poets

Who go and go to woods to see poems

Or what they've been told are poems

And die in them, their poems, all

The poems they have left in the woods.

Feelings We Haven't Had

Before I was thinking in poems, I was

thinking in lighthouses, I mean the way a

light can spin.

East Greenwich is nowhere but a memory for

sea, and a light can turn in any good

direction

and come back again with eyes turned

inward like the dead have eyes turned

inward so that

they might see themselves forever without

having to be bothered by other people's pale

or purple faces and so much bad art. There

was snow. There was snow over East

Greenwich when I first went out for light-

houses, sparked or naked in their standing by the

sea. (This is the little city where ships are

mended or at least talked out of throwing

their men into the sea.)

I, too, was busy standing by the sea, but I

would not think in poems the way I had been

told to

all those mornings in dead relatives'

thatched houses. Because to think in poems

when standing

near the ocean meant to give in and forgive

the fallen sailors who had gone into the

ocean

and drowned there, sailors who for all their

time spent swimming must have wanted to

be dead.

Anyway, that's what they said. So I went out

near the ocean, walking foggy through the

snow, and called

O Little Ship! O Ocean! But no dead man

would rise to acknowledge my

forgiveness

because, as it were, he did not feel the need

to be forgiven, at least in times of quickly

coming

snow. A stranger said that if I were not too

clumsy to go further toward the slippery cliff

I could see

whales when they come carrying their old air

up from the faraway black insides of the sea –

so naturally I did and so did he. He didn't

want to make me into some good poem, but

he also did not know a thing about predicting

whales. We two of us had pale

and purple faces, so we left one another on

same but separate rocks and went back to

looking lonely

out toward sea. Did I tell you what bad art I
can be called into? Somewhere behind me always,
as small as East Greenwich, there is the light.

Pele and Io

I am a guest in any home that might be mine.
I fill you, moon, set loose as you were to
wander the drowsy earth as a beast, a present
of presents to

angering gods you might have touched in
pity or lust. I fill you now to explosion. What
maidens of sulfuric compounds are we, we
who have hands

for unbuttoning blouses and untying shoe
laces without damning the men who would
have us in songs of praise or wonder. There
is no such thing

as love. We've been stung and stung into
black madness. I fill you, moon; I know you.
If my hundred eyes could sleep, I'd dream
you circling the giants

in your white gown, unwedded, in the dream

state of some Galilean prophecy. All the men

and mechanisms geared to touch you would

be ash in

my best crater. I fill you, moon; I've found

you tangled in my hair. I know each where

you've traveled inside and when you orbit

backwards,

trusting sky on sky to catch you should you

break off into that dark spot that splits your

reddest, blushing rings. I, too, have felt the

touch that ruins

a steady surface temperature and sparks a

spiral. I, too, have slept in hospitals for

heartbreak. When I last filled you, moon, my

lover was awake and

dreaming murder. He made his dive into the

ashy middles of what remains after a fire.

I've made a list for reckoning the distance

kept between a moon

and the object that it orbits. I've melted

down the metals of telescopes and telephones

to know the heat it takes to tear a

man from his own body. I've

been the beach that takes the beating and the

waves that drown whole cities block by

block. The touch of tides is what drives you,

moon, away and farther

from the mouths of gods and each decade of

their radioactive decay. I fill you, moon. I am

a visitor as far as any blood or bone may be. I

construct the inner

fires of a lovesick afternoon, in which you

chance a look of sun against a man's smooth

and freckled shoulders until time tells to

turn yourself to wander.

Someone Go Ahead and Swap Our Oceans Again

I boil one dull hurricane for everyone

whose in-between girl I've been. Not

good enough even for fire. In the bathtub

is where the waves start, simple at first

in the bubble-mist. I shave my legs. I mean

I pull your chest hair out of me, skin after

skin. It chokes smoky in the drain, not good

enough even to burn. In the blue sheets

I make a blue dress and won't be skin.

A wind. I twirl and twirl that suffocating wind.

Between the sea and me I wouldn't dare you –

softening intestine filled for sand. Soft-

haired girls not good enough even for smoke.

Under the skylight is where I swallow the bird,

first drowned bird of nighttime, and let its beak

in me. Let its sharp beak. Rain begins all the

unanimous sound. I mean I'm set for breaking

into you. I mean I'm set. Not good enough even

for ash in glass dishes. Not good enough for

bringing anything back to the ground.

The Streets May Turn to Paper Suddenly

I am neither shadow nor wife. I have no hand

for painting

flowers nor how they fill any room or bed-

spread or plate

of meats for guests who come to fill my

house and how

that happens. How unlucky to have a secret,

women, how

unlucky it is to have. I have one broken

finger

still but am no wife. Check through these

windows at my

winter leaves: they are green with life. This

pill-by-pill makes one

book and cowers. And so we are at home

together, after hours.

Moon Storm

I send my specter out to find me,
my other specter. I like to think I split

exactly in the middle, but what symmetry
would that be? There is no even

landmass I have traveled upon;
not in spring, honey, as you promised.

There are two of you for my two hands:
I forgive you. I am announcing how to kiss

in your first ever dream – let all the
disappearing happen at once. I am sitting inside

one of you for a while. I am sitting inside
another me. In a little thunder

I send my specter out and find me,
moon-hung, cloudy, uneven yet for traveling

a landmass, the dumbstruck dream

I have traveled in before.

ACKNOWLEDGEMENTS

For Sylvia Plath's "Three Women" and Juan Rulfo's "Macario," stolen and worked here.

Various poems included herein have previously appeared in: *Artifice, Banango Street, Dancing Girl Press, Ilk, MOPE Musings, The Scrambler, Sundog Lit, Sway Press, Thrush, Thunderclap!*, and *Vomit*.

OTHER WORKS BY KAT DIXON

BOOKS

TEMPORARY YES, poems

HERE/OTHER, a novella

GIRL IN POEM, poems & essays

CHAPBOOKS

KISSISSIPPI, poems

PLANETARY MASS, poems

DON'T GO FISH, poems

BIRDING, poems